CW01238261

Original title:
Trapped in the Dance of Illusion

Copyright © 2025 Creative Arts Management OÜ
All rights reserved.

Author: Nolan Kingsley
ISBN HARDBACK: 978-3-69081-458-4
ISBN PAPERBACK: 978-3-69081-954-1

Lies Beneath the Surface

Beneath the smiles and laughter's cheer,
A jester's mask hides every fear.
In shadows cast by dreams absurd,
We twirl along, unheard, unheard.

With every step, we take the bait,
In a carnival of fickle fate.
The mirror jokes at our expense,
While we dance on, lost in pretense.

Motionless in a Spinning World

Round and round, the music plays,
We flail our arms in clumsy ways.
The ground appears to move away,
As we giggle through the fray.

Like marionettes with tangled strings,
A game of joy that chaos brings.
We freeze in spins and make a fuss,
While sanity rides the crazy bus.

Fragments of Unreality

Puppets dance on dreams so bright,
While truths are tucked away from sight.
In a kaleidoscope of weird delight,
We prance around the foolish night.

A laugh erupts from silly slips,
As gravity plays its joker tricks.
Underneath this painted scene,
We jesters know what might have been.

Caught in the Delusive Waltz

Two left feet in a three-step glide,
We waddle on with playful pride.
Each twirl reveals the flaws we hide,
In this fun-house where dreams deride.

The floor spins like a pancake flopped,
As laughter soars, and worries dropped.
We mime our way to the final bow,
In this illusion, we wonder how.

Glimmers of Forgotten Steps

In a world of swirling skirts,
I step on toes with flair,
The music plays, I'm just a blur,
While laughter fills the air.

Twinkle toes and clumsy feet,
I spin as if on ice,
With every turn, I lose my grip,
But hey, it feels so nice!

A waltz of giggles, back and forth,
No rhythm found in me,
I can't recall the moves I learned,
Yet still, I dance with glee.

So join this quirky slip and slide,
We'll laugh until we drop,
In this jest of joyous twirls,
The silliness won't stop!

The Choreography of Shadows

Footsteps echo in the dark,
As shadows start to prance,
I mimic every twist and turn,
But miss the final chance.

A ghostly spin, a phantom leap,
My partner's just a wall,
With every laugh I tumble down,
In this delightful sprawl.

Puppeteered by flickering lights,
I dance a silly jig,
In the corner, shadows sway,
While I just spin and gig.

Tonight, the floor is made of dreams,
A stage of playful night,
Each jig a joke, each dip a grin,
In the absence of the light.

A Dance with Eclipsed Memories

I stumble through a twilight haze,
With moves I seldom know,
Each twist a blur, each sway a crash,
Oh, what a flashy show!

Forgotten steps in ancient grooves,
I fumble like a clown,
While echoes of the past ring loud,
I trip and tumble down.

In shadows where the memories lurk,
A misstep leads to sparks,
From laughter born of awkward sways,
As the night sings and barks.

So let the music play, my friend,
And let our spirits rise,
For even in the goofiest dance,
We find the sweetest sighs!

Curves of Unseen Realities

In circles spun with whimsy's grace,
I glide on air, or so it seems,
With each misstep, an artful fall,
Reality's a pile of dreams.

A twist here, a flick there,
It's all a little wild,
But in this game of make-believe,
I'm still the giggling child.

Round and round, the edges blur,
With laughter chasing close,
In this loop of light and shade,
I find the fun I chose.

So sway along the wobbly line,
Embrace the crazy beat,
For in the curves of unseen fates,
Life's dance is quite a treat!

Swaying Between Reality and Reverie

In a world where socks can't find a pair,
My feet twist left while my thoughts go where?
A cat in a hat sings a tune offbeat,
While I step on my own two left feet.

Mirrors reflect a dance of the absurd,
I trip on my tongue, forgetting each word.
The floor is a trampoline, bouncy and bright,
As I bounce back to sanity, oh what a sight!

The ceiling hums with whispers of jest,
As I attempt to waltz, it's a comical mess.
I laugh with the shadows that giggle and play,
While the clock ticks on, leading me astray.

In this circus of dreams, I'm the jester supreme,
With a wobble and twirl, I create my own theme.
So let's whirl in this picnic of whimsical glee,
Forever chasing mirages that dance just for me.

A Jigsaw of Colliding Shadows

Pieces of puzzles are scattered around,
Each corner a chuckle, with nonsense unbound.
My feet twist and turn like a playful charade,
While the shadows all laugh, in a whimsical parade.

A kaleidoscope giggle spins stories so bold,
As I juggle lost marbles of silver and gold.
Each thought is a dancer, each laugh a refrain,
As I waltz with confusion, my own silly brain.

In a room full of mirrors, reflections collide,
I can't find my left, maybe it's my right side.
With a leap and a twirl, I chase after my hat,
While the walls throw confetti, aren't they just fat?

So here in this riddle where shadows entwine,
The laughter keeps ringing, it's all so divine.
As I stumble through fragments, a jigsaw of cheer,
Let's dance with the quirks, for there's nothing to fear.

Whispers in a Twirling Dream

In a world where socks don't match,
And the moon's a wobbly ball,
We trip on our toes, then dash,
Through walls that giggle and sprawl.

The chairs they dance, quite bold,
With jigs that make no sense,
I twirl and whirl on glitter gold,
While logic takes a vacation hence.

Laughter hides in every sweep,
As floors become a slide,
We tumble down in silly heaps,
With stars our silly guide.

In this realm, we skip and sing,
While dreams wear clownish frowns,
Every spin's a cheerful sting,
In our merry, topsy-turvy towns.

Shadows on the Stage

Under a light that flickers bright,
The actors fumble their lines,
With capes that wrap around so tight,
And shoes that squeak like pines.

The villain trips, the hero falls,
A pie flies through the air,
With each mishap, the laughter calls,
As chaos fills the square.

"Look at me," the jester sighs,
With a hat askew and bent,
Embracing all our foolish cries,
In scripted accidents, we're sent.

As shadows dance, the label's wrong,
We laugh at every twist,
For life's a most ridiculous song,
And joy is hard to resist.

Chasing Flickers of Fantasy

A rumor floats on whispered breeze,
That unicorns love to play,
We chase them through the tangled trees,
While giggles lead the way.

A dragon sips its tea with grace,
In a hat that's far too wide,
As fairies make a grand chess race,
With dancing frogs beside.

We stumble over roots that laugh,
While clouds wear goofy frowns,
In this realm, we lose the path,
And twirl in silly rounds.

Chasing gleams that flit and sway,
We find ourselves confused,
Yet every misstep, every play,
Leaves hearts happily bruised.

The Ballet of Deceit

With grace, they leap and spin around,
In slippers meant for swans,
Yet one must dodge the painted ground,
Where good sense clearly yawns.

A pirouette turns into falls,
While tutus trip and fray,
Each pose becomes a laughing call,
In this silly ballet.

Here's a case of mistook shoes,
A left for right and back,
The dancer shimmies, laughs, and woos,
In a dazzling, awkward act.

We cheer for all the pratfalls grand,
As elegance takes flight,
In a dance where strange dreams expand,
And whimsy laughs all night.

A Curtain Call for the Misguided

In the spotlight, they prance and twirl,
Not a clue in this dizzy whirl.
Marionettes in threads of fate,
Laughing loud, they hesitate.

With each step, a stumble grows,
Tangled in their shining clothes.
The audience roars, a comical sight,
As they dance into the night.

Oh, take a bow, you foolish few,
Lost in a web of dreams askew.
Chasing shadows, a merry chase,
In a carnival of silliness and grace.

So here's to the fools, the jester's kin,
Playing the game, where none can win.
With a wink and a laugh, they flip the script,
In the circus of life, they're well-equipped.

The Rhythm of Ephemeral Dreams

Bouncing on clouds of candy floss,
With each leap, they face a loss.
Tickling stars with silly hats,
Waltzing with imaginary cats.

What's one step or a little fall?
Echoing giggles in the hall.
Hopping lights with glee abound,
Finding joy where lost dreams are found.

A jigsaw of hopes, still in play,
In a tune that wobbles away.
Cups of laughter, spinning fast,
Holding tight to a future cast.

So dance, my friend, with all your might,
In the dim glow of twinkling light.
For the rhythm may bend, but never break,
In a waltz of wonder, make no mistake.

Traces of Forgotten Visions

A jumbled map of dreams in flight,
Chasing shadows in the night.
Giggles flicker, oh, what a tease,
Pants falling, makes everyone wheeze!

With hopscotch stars above their heads,
Tangled in mischief, they tread.
A blur of colors, a frosty cheer,
Bouncing back, they have no fear.

Oh, to dance on the edge of reason,
Each turn marks a different season.
Whirling dervishes of thought,
In this jive of woes, they're caught.

So here's to the merry band,
With a wink, they take a stand.
For in their missteps, joy ignites,
Crafting laughter from their flights.

Echoes of an Illusory Embrace

In a swirl of flustered delight,
Fumbling makes a comical sight.
They trip and twirl, but what's the gain?
Catching giggles as they feign.

A tango with shadows, bold yet shy,
In this frolic, they will fly.
Hand in hand, they spin around,
Lost in laughter, joy unbound.

Who needs a map to lead the way?
When whimsy is the game they play.
With every bobble, hearts expand,
In this circus, they make their stand.

So grab a partner and take a chance,
In this effusive, silly dance.
With echoes fading, yet sweetly bright,
They'll waltz through dreams into the night.

The Riddle of Twisted Steps

In a party where my feet go wild,
I step left, and then I'm beguiled.
A spin here, a twirl there,
Oh look! I'm dancing in midair!

The rhythm sways, I trip and fall,
A jester's laugh, oh how we enthrall!
Each step's a riddle, a puzzling feat,
With footwear that's not made for the street!

Spin me round, I'm dizzy, oh dear!
My shadow's chuckling, "This is sheer!"
Wobble and wiggle, we all collide,
In this merry mess, let laughter glide!

So here's to the dance that's one big jest,
With every misstep, we're surely blessed!
Raise a glass to the wobbling prance,
In this riddle, we all must dance!

Velvet Chains of Seduction

A glimpse of velvet, smooth and sly,
Whispers sweet beneath the sky.
With each pull, I'm wound up tight,
In chains of charm, I'm lost tonight!

The sparkles flash, oh what a tease,
"Tug a little more," says temptation with ease.
My heart's a drum, beats out of control,
In this velvety game, I've sold my soul!

With every tug, I giggle, I frown,
These fancy chains don't weigh me down.
They dance and sway, oh what fun!
In this gilded trap, I'm never done!

So here's to velvet, smooth and bold,
In the laugh of love, let stories be told.
Though bound by silk, I'll not complain,
For in this jig, there's joy—no pain!

Mirage of Forbidden Whispers

In a garden where secrets bloom,
Whispers float like sweet perfume.
A giggle here, a shush goes there,
In this mirage, we play the air!

Promises hang, like fruit on a tree,
Each one more juicy, a taste of glee.
But plug your ears, don't be a fool,
For whispers dance outside the school!

Each laugh a phantom, a glimmer bright,
Chasing shadows into the night.
With every giggle, a secret will flow,
Can we trust what we don't really know?

So let's toast to whispers, softly spun,
In the ballet of jest, we've all won.
As we twirl 'round in this playful trance,
In the mirage, we take our chance!

The Serenade of False Hopes

A song that flutters, light as a breeze,
Promises linger, just like tease.
"We'll dance all night," the tune does say,
Yet morning steals the night away!

In bows of hope, we twine and sway,
Each note a wish that won't decay.
With every chord, my heart takes flight,
Oh what a serenade, pure delight!

Yet as the music softens and fades,
Reality peeks through the masquerades.
But laughter bursts through the hopeful song,
In this serenade, we all belong!

So let's sing of hopes that rise and fall,
In this comedy, we'll stand tall.
With jest and cheer, we'll take our stand,
For false hopes make this life so grand!

The Spiral Staircase of Reflection

Round and round, I climb with glee,
Each mirror shows a clown to me.
The stairs, they twist, they bend and sway,
I laugh aloud, then trip and play.

With each new view, my hair's a mess,
A funky style, I must confess.
Upward leads to downward fights,
In this waltz of silly heights.

Shadows dance, they tease and prance,
A jester's jig, a confused romance.
I spin and twirl, a dizzy throng,
In a world where I belong.

At last, the top, I reach my fate,
A mirror ball reflects my state.
In this funhouse, I do declare,
I'm all alone, but who would care?

Ethereal Steps in the Fog

In the mist, I skip and hop,
While unseen friends all laugh and stop.
Each step I take feels out of time,
A waltz with weeds, a silly rhyme.

I whisper secrets to the haze,
It giggles back in cheeky ways.
Through hidden paths, I chase a jive,
Through smoky dreams, I feel alive.

The ground below, a squishy sound,
Each clumsy move, I spin around.
The fog won't tell if I'm lost,
Just keeps me light, no matter the cost.

With every turn, it's all a tease,
Oh sweet confusion, such a breeze.
In this fun-clad, misty show,
I dance with shadows, rob and crow.

The Labyrinth of Façades

In a maze of masks, I stroll with flair,
In every turn, a different pair.
I wear a grin, the joker's craft,
While wandering through this silly draft.

Each wall I tap brings giggles near,
As echoes blend with raucous cheer.
A jester's hat, a wig askew,
In this charade, what's false is true.

The pathways twist, they beckon me,
With paths of giggles, wait and see.
A dance of roles, we all can play,
In this grand scheme, we find our way.

So come and join the masquerade,
As laughter blooms, the doubts will fade.
In the labyrinth's hold, we'll find a way,
To turn our frowns to a lighter sway.

A Tangle of Ghostly Dances

The specters swirl with grace and glide,
In foggy gowns, they twist and slide.
With goofy grins, they pull me near,
Together we'll unleash some cheer.

Boo! They shout, then jig about,
As I join in, I dance without doubt.
In this community of ghostly limbs,
We twirl and spin, our fate it brims.

A poltergeist leads in a disco beat,
While the shadows stomp with whimsical feet.
With each odd step, the giggles grow,
In this ghoulish dance, we steal the show.

As we weave through space, a tangled jest,
Haunted humor feels like the best.
In a waltz that's silly and slightly absurd,
We chase our fears, unheard, unheard.

Cascading Lies on the Floor

Once I thought I knew it all,
Reality took a funny fall.
With every spin, the truth will veer,
Like a pair of socks, oh dear!

They say the floors have tales to tell,
But all I hear is a ringing bell.
Puppets grin with strings all frayed,
As we twirl in this masquerade.

Confetti bursts, a colorful mess,
Each truth feels like a funny guess.
A cat in boots, dancing so spry,
Makes me wonder, oh me, oh my!

The music plays, a jolly tune,
We spin around like a cartoon.
Each laugh echoes, a joyful lore,
In the chaos, we dance some more.

Waltzing with the Unattainable

In the midst of a quirky waltz,
The unattainable takes a twirl that exalts.
I chase my dreams with a comical flair,
But they float away, like a puff of air.

Around I go with a hapless grin,
Dodging reality, where to begin?
Oh look! A jester joins the scene,
And all my hopes wear a pointed green.

A partner steps on my unsuspecting toes,
The rhythm's wild; everybody knows!
With each misstep, I try to glide,
But laughter erupts; I swing and slide.

Together we spin, a farcical plight,
Chasing shadows that vanish from sight.
In this waltz, the humor's divine,
As we laugh at the line, so hard to define.

The Dance of Fractured Lights

Through prisms bright, we stumble about,
A jig for fools is all we shout.
With every step, the shadows play,
Making light of night and day.

Reflecting bits of broken dreams,
We tiptoe past in whimsical seams.
Flickering hopes whirl like fireflies,
While reality laughs with sarcastic sighs.

A disco ball made of shattered glass,
Throws glimmers on the faces that pass.
With every twirl, a chuckle's released,
As the glow shows the inner beast.

In this silly dance of fractured charms,
We sway and giggle, oblivious to qualms.
Chasing glimmers, oh what a sight,
With fractured lights, we dance through the night.

Entering the Realm of Half-Truths

A door swings wide to a world odd,
Filled with riddles of truth, quite flawed.
Each half-smile tells a quirky tale,
As the logic starts to set sail.

Oh, how we strut in our playground of quirks,
Where lemons become magical lurks.
With each step, a giggle escapes,
Amidst tangled paths and funny shapes.

The mirrors here are surely jesters,
Reflecting shadows, silly testers.
In this realm, we dance like dreams,
Entwined in laughter, bursting seams.

So come, take part in this frolicsome spree,
Where half-truths glide, oh so carefree.
Each chuckle spins a tale worn,
In the realm where confusion is born.

A Ballet of Misplaced Dreams

In a tutu made of paper, they sway,
Twisting their feet in a comical way.
The music is silent, loud and bold,
As they prance in patterns, a sight to behold.

A pirouette here, a stumble there,
Their partners are pillows, floating in air.
With each graceful fall, they laugh and they cheer,
Conducting an orchestra only they hear.

The stage is a kitchen, the spotlight a pan,
They leap over dishes, as only they can.
With spaghetti strings tied to each toe,
They twirl 'til they topple, all go with the flow.

In dreams of perfection, they spin and they glide,
But only to wind up on their laughter ride.
Through salads and soufflés, the fun never ends,
In their ballet of blunders, they dance 'round as friends.

The Tangle of Twisted Threads

A needle in hand, but fashion's a mess,
Stitching together a most foolish dress.
The fabric is wrinkled, colors askew,
But oh, the delight in this quilt of taboo!

With threads made of giggles and sequins so bright,
They tumble and fall under disco ball light.
Each twist of the fabric is met with a grin,
As they stitch up their tales of misfortune and spin.

Their outfits are odd, a patchwork of dreams,
With mismatched buttons and whimsical seams.
The audience roars with laughter and cheer,
At this fashion show filled with faux pas and cheer!

In the tangle of yarns, they find their delight,
Creating catwalks that gleam in the night.
For who needs a runway when chaos is fun?
In this quirky parade, they've already won!

Queries in a Tattered Tutu

What's that in the corner? A lost ballet shoe?
Or did someone mistake it for breakfast stew?
With questions and giggles, they dance through the room,

In tutus of paper, as flowers all bloom.

With pirouettes that lead into fits of glee,
They ponder the meaning of 'who's on the tree?'
Their partners are cats, and their audience, mice,
Where the rules of the stage are a roll of the dice.

Why do roses smell lovely while cabbages groan?
With each clumsy leap, some wisdom is shown.
Between silly socks and a crumpled tiara,
They waltz through confusion—a glorious era.

Each query they ask is wrapped in a joke,
While their feet keep on moving and hearts gently choke.
In this whimsical world where laughter's the creed,
They inquire about life while living it, freed!

The Mirage of the Quiet Melodies

In the still of the night, when silence is loud,
They dance under starlight, gathering a crowd.
But the tune is a phantom, elusive and shy,
Yet their feet keep on tapping—it's hard to deny.

They sway with a flair for concocting a beat,
While potato chip crumbs dance under their feet.
The notes are imaginary, yet they keep time,
In this ballet of whimsy, they feel so sublime.

With the moon as their witness, they laugh at the air,
As their shadows all whisper, "What's going on where?"
The melody hums, like a popcorn surprise,
As they giggle and glide, under starlit skies.

In mirages of laughter, they find their delight,
As dreamers of nonsense, they twirl through the night.
For melodies quiet fill hearts in a dance,
In this swirling escapade, they leap and romance!

The Dance Within the Veil

Behind a curtain, shadows sway,
In pajamas, we twirl and play.
Chasing giggles, lost in flight,
We hop and skip 'til day turns night.

Whispers of laughter fill the air,
A waltz of glee, without a care.
Clumsy steps on the wooden floor,
A tango with the kitchen door.

Invisible partners, spin around,
As socks slide on with screeching sound.
What's reality? Oh, who can tell?
We glide in chaos, all is well!

With jigs and jests, we lose the lane,
In the masquerade, we go insane.
Fools in the night, we jiggle and bounce,
In this merry mess, we laugh and pounce.

Swirls of Evasive Graces

Waltzing through dreams that slip away,
Like cats in a hat, we dance and sway.
A pirouette of pancake spills,
As jellybeans meet dapper frills.

Round we go, with squeals of cheer,
Dodging the chores, in silly gear.
Prancing lightly on bubblegum feet,
Each mishap a reason for more retreat.

Juggling thoughts like wayward balloons,
We leap through rooms with goofy tunes.
In the mirror, we prance and pout,
In this funhouse where truth's played out.

Glimpses of wisdom twirl and glide,
While candy-coated truths collide.
With all the twists and playful bends,
We laugh away as laughter transcends.

A Soirée with the Unseen

Beneath the stars, we host a ball,
With chairs that giggle and walls that stall.
Invisible guests all take a seat,
As they chatter softly and tap their feet.

Plates filled high with secrets untold,
We dance to rhythms of tales bold.
A conga line, where shadows parade,
With quirks and jests, we serenade.

The chandelier sways with a smirk,
As we share tales of our silly quirks.
Confetti made of fleeting dreams,
In this whirlwind, nothing's as it seems.

So let's sway with whimsy in tow,
Under the moon's curious glow.
In laughter's embrace, we spin and dive,
In this revelry, we feel alive.

The Ballet of Yearning and Doubt

Echoes of hope perform a tease,
In ruffled skirts and scoffing breeze.
We leap with dreams that tie and twist,
In the waltz of wishes none can resist.

A ballet of quirks, perhaps a mess,
With plucky hearts that rarely rest.
Fumbles and tumbles fill our play,
As we dance the doubts of the day.

Glances exchanged in a twinkling glance,
With a shuffle that's more than chance.
In this vibrant act, skeptics cheer,
As we pirouette on hopes sincere.

With a flourish, we bow to the crowd,
In giggles of freedom, joyful and loud.
Unveiling the charm in every clout,
We find the joy in yearning and doubt.

The Unraveling of Delusional Threads

In a world where socks mate in pairs,
The cat knows secrets, yet hardly shares.
A jester juggles thoughts out of sight,
Chasing shadows in the flickering light.

Every misstep's a giggle, a cheer,
Spinning tales that twist, bend, and veer.
What's real? What's fake? A wobbly ride,
On this carousel, we all must abide.

The puzzle's a picture of scrambled glee,
With pieces so playful, they dance in spree.
A rainbow whispers jokes in the breeze,
While time pirouettes, teasing with ease.

Laughter bounces where wisdom would tread,
As daydreams trip over visions long dead.
In this circus of quirks, we shuffle and sway,
Embracing the whimsy, come what may!

Enchantment in a Broken Prism

In shades of laughter, colors collide,
A banana peel rests where dreams reside.
The moonwears glasses, half-full, half-wild,
While wisdom winks, a mischievous child.

Reflecting confusion, light bends and spins,
Reality chuckles as nonsense begins.
A ballerina tripping on invisible threads,
Dances with daisies, tilting her heads.

The world's a sketch made in crayon and glee,
Where nothing is what it seems to be.
With whispers of magic, the playful unmask,
And truth hides in corners—what a task!

Oh, the cackles we gather in wobbly shoes,
As they spin silly tales of which we can't choose.
In this fractured spectrum, twirls intertwine,
Creating a vision that's utterly fine!

Steps in the Hall of Shadows

Oh, the echoes that bounce in the dim-lit hall,
Where ghosts of mischief begin their brawl.
The shadows conspire in a giggly dance,
With every footfall, a chance for romance.

Twisting and turning, they glide with glee,
Tripping on stories we dare not foresee.
A hiccuping candle that flickers for fun,
As laughter escapes like a thief on the run.

In this game of hide and sneak, we whirl,
Invisible partners in a wobbly twirl.
Each step a giggle, a small, silly bluff,
As the echoing hall reminds us: it's tough!

Through corridors painted in whims and light,
We stumble in rhythm, losing all fright.
The nights are for dancing, embracing our jest,
In the luxurious chaos, we find all the best!

The Carnival of Reflected Souls

Welcome to the circus, where reflections play,
In mirrors of laughter, we tumble away.
A unicyclist juggles dreams with a grin,
While popcorn clouds bubble, inviting us in.

The ticket booth grins—a cheeky delight,
As the wise old owl winks in the night.
Each carnival game, a twist of the mind,
Where fun reigns supreme, and logic's maligned.

On the Ferris wheel spins, a riddle of cheer,
With echoes of giggles, it pulls us near.
Each ride whispers secrets of friendship and fate,
In this carnival glow, we celebrate late.

Let's flip our illusions on this merry-go-round,
In the laughter of souls, true joy can be found.
With humor so bright, we dance in the flame,
At the carnival's heart, we're all still the same!

The Waltz of Fractured Realities

In a hall of mirrors, we prance and spin,
Each reflection a stranger, don't know where to begin.
My left foot says yes, while my right foot says no,
In this absurd ballet, it's a comical show.

The tempo of nonsense takes hold of the floor,
I step on a toe, then I tango with snore.
The music's a jigsaw, yet we play along,
With giggles and stumbles, we sing out of song.

Partners with shadows, we twirl 'round the light,
A flurry of color, it's a marvelous sight.
The lead keeps on fading, the follow just trips,
With laughter as currency, we fund our missteps.

A one-two cha-cha, then slip on a shoe,
The rhythm of folly is carried anew.
In this dance of bemusement, we'll spin 'til we're done,
With smiles as our trophies, we've already won.

Illumination Beneath the Gossamer

Under lights that flicker like fireflies at play,
I waltz with a ghost who won't let me sway.
Her dress made of shadows, she's light as a breeze,
We chuckle at fate as we twirl 'neath the trees.

Each step is a riddle, each spin a new plot,
What's real and what's fake? Oh, who really forgot?
A hand on my shoulder? Oh wait, it's the air!
But dancing with nothing? I haven't a care!

The gossamer threads weave my path like a maze,
I zigzag through memories lost in a haze.
I trip over laughter, I tumble on glee,
My partner, a whisper, just chuckles with me.

In this magical room where the silly collide,
We dance as though nobody's taken a side.
With each bob and swerve, I can feel my heart race,
Under illusions that charm, there's just joy in our pace.

The Riddle within the Rumba

A conundrum of choreography without a clear end,
My hips tell a secret, yet my feet seem to bend.
Why is my partner a mirror in disguise?
In this quirky conundrum, no one's truly wise.

As we tango with riddles, the audience laughs,
With every misstep, we add to our gaffes.
The light hits our faces like confetti on dreams,
We prance through the puzzles, or so it seems.

The double entendres take center stage now,
While the lead tries to follow, we wiggle and vow.
With a wink and a nod, we embrace the whim,
Caught in a rumba where senses grow dim.

Now twirling on questions, we giggle and spin,
A dance so perplexing, we forget where we've been.
With riddles unraveling, our laughter takes flight,
In this joyous enigma, we dance through the night!

Flickering Lights of the Inconstant Stage

The spotlight's a trickster, it dances away,
While I curtsy to shadows that choose not to stay.
Each flash tells a story, but none is the same,
In this playful charade, we're all part of the game.

Flickering lights, like thoughts, twist and abide,
With rhythms that shift like a wily old tide.
The floor is a puzzle, and I'm solving with style,
Every moment a chuckle, each misstep worth while.

With a giggle and grin, I sway toward the night,
While colors collide in a fabulous sight.
We're actors and jesters, in costumes of cheer,
In a play that confounds, but our hearts lead us here.

As the curtain descends, I laugh with the crowd,
In the flickering glow, let my folly be loud.
For in moments of whimsy, the world finds its grace,
In the laughter of light, we're all part of the chase.

Traces of an Elusive Pulse

In a room full of jest, we sway and spin,
With shoes made of rubber and laughs from within.
The music is loud, yet we're out of step,
Two left feet and a giggle, oh what a rep!

A twirl here, a stumble, we dance with glee,
Onlookers chuckle; 'Is that you or me?'
Whispers of rhythm drown in the fun,
As we chase shadows, our game has begun!

Imitating swans, but we're all ducks,
With feathers of giggles and hiccupping sucks.
We leap over puddles that splash us in jest,
In the waltz of our whimsy, we know we're the best!

As the lights start to fade and music will cease,
We dance to the laughter, our hearts are in peace.
And though we're a mess, we embrace every fall,
In this crazy charade, we've captured it all!

The Memorandum of a Lost Dance

A missed step here, a hop over there,
With glittery shoes, we float in the air.
The memo is lost, the instructions unclear,
While we whirl through the chaos, no need for a seer!

To the left, to the right, we're giggling wide,
Our moves like balloons, on a wild, windy ride.
Yet somehow we manage to float with such grace,
A silly parade in this fanciful space!

In this video game of invisible walls,
Our avatars clash with comical brawls.
Each twirl is a yawn, as we leap through the air,
With faces so funny, we simply don't care!

The curtains are closing, the lights start to dim,
But the echoes of laughter will never grow dim.
So here's to the folly, the steps misconstrued,
In the record of nonsense, we're blissfully skewed!

Magician's Illusionary Waltz

A top hat appears, full of giggles and tricks,
As we shuffle and wiggle, no pattern, just kicks.
With rabbits that hop into shoes out of sight,
We dance around tables that wobble with fright!

The cards all confound in a colorful mess,
While our feet find the rhythm, we're bound to impress.
It's a curious chaos, but how we do prance,
In a world of illusions, we take our chance!

With mirrors reflecting our goofy charade,
Each thought is a jest, every notion displayed.
While the audience gasps, we giggle away,
In this farcical gala, it's all just play!

As the final act nears and the audience roars,
We bow with a flourish, slipping out through the doors.
In the haze of our laughter, we leave a bright trail,
From the magic of nonsense, we will never bail!

Fabric of Fantasies Weaving

With threads of our laughter, we stitch through the night,
In patterns of whimsy, everything's bright.
We spin and we twirl, 'neath the stars' playful glow,
In the fabric of dreams, our wild colors flow!

The loom of the universe grins as we play,
Its needles entwined in our clumsy ballet.
Each stitch, a mishap; yet it's all so divine,
Creating a tale that's delightfully mine!

A tapestry woven of giggles and cheer,
Where every misstep brings a friend ever near.
As we fashion our story with threads that entwine,
We dance in the fabric, and everything's fine!

With each silly jig, we create what's our own,
As the fabric of life is fantastically sewn.
We'll prance on forever, with laughter our trade,
In a world filled with color, our joy is displayed!

When Reality Sways

Reality wobbles, a jester's delight,
We dip and twirl, under starlight bright.
With socks mismatched and shoes too tight,
We laugh at the shadows that dance out of sight.

The world spins round like a topsy-top,
Each move a question, a hiccup, a bop.
In a carnival mirror, we twist and swap,
Finding joy in the slip, not wanting to stop.

A laugh erupts as we stumble and fumble,
The rhythm escapes, but we never grumble.
With each funny fall, our doubts gently crumble,
In this mad caper, we cheer for the jumble.

So pull on those shoes and let's join the throng,
We'll dance on the edge of the silly and wrong.
Sweeping up giggles, we'll sing our own song,
In this wobbly whirl, we feel we belong.

Treading on Illusive Paths

On a path made of dreams, we stumble along,
With each sneaky twist, nothing seems wrong.
We step on the clouds while belting a song,
Pretending to know where we all really belong.

With ribbons of nonsense tied around our feet,
We shuffle through puddles in a loose beat.
The world's a soft carpet, surprisingly neat,
As we twirl through the laughter, with no need to cheat.

Mirrorball reflections sprinkle the ground,
As tricks play their parts, behind scenes abound.
Outsmarting our minds in a dance so profound,
We find our own rhythm in the silliness found.

Through whims of the heart, we sway to the light,
The fun in the farce makes every wrong right.
With twinkling delight, we'll dance into night,
On paths made of giggles, our spirits take flight.

The Ghosts of Past Choreographies

The phantoms of moves we forget to recall,
They prance and they laugh while we stumble and fall.
In the spotlight's embrace, we give it our all,
But the steps are outdated, like wallpaper, they sprawl.

A tap of the toe leads to an awkward spin,
Like stepping on grapes with a cheeky grin.
The past gives a wink, then it pulls us right in,
As we shuffle with spirits and try to begin.

With echoes of laughter reverberating loud,
The ghosts of the dance break out from the crowd.
In a mishmash of joy, we're both silly and proud,
Creating a chaos that, wow, it's a shroud.

So let's trip over time with gleeful dismay,
The folly of steps, oh, what fun to display.
In the tangled embrace, we'll surely outplay,
The ghosts of old dances that led us astray.

Underneath the Glittering Surface

Beneath the glam, the chaos unfolds,
As we giggle and wiggle, the story is told.
With sparkles a-shimmer and antics so bold,
The truth hides in laughter, pure joy to behold.

The stage may be fancy, a dazzling show,
But beneath the allurement, the fun starts to grow.
With flailing and laughter, we steal the glow,
In the mist of the madness, we learn how to flow.

With splashes of color and confetti in air,
Every captured moment is a tease of despair.
Yet we leap and we roll, without a care,
Creating a joyride, a whimsical flair.

So lift up your glass, let's toast to the art,
The spark in our souls, where the antics do start.
With a wink and a twirl, we play every part,
Underneath the glimmer, it's joy that we chart.

Slivers of a Distant Truth

Caught in a swirl of glittery dreams,
Frogs dance in hats, or so it seems.
With laughter they leap, as the moon does wink,
While wise owls ponder, and squirrels just blink.

Chasing shadows, all in a blur,
Tiptoeing lightly on soft, sweet purr.
The truth wears a mask, oh what a jest,
While giggles emerge from an uninvited guest.

Bubbles float high, they pop with a sound,
Each burst brings a giggle that circles around.
Silly the ways the mind plays its tricks,
As clouds form shapes in fantastic flicks.

So let's twirl in circles, the music so grand,
With jellybean partners in a soft, warm sand.
The ribbons of farce, a colorful spree,
In slivers of moments, we dance and we flee.

The Mirage of Yearning's Call

In fields where hotcakes grow like flowers,
The bakery hums, oh what powers!
Scones wear scarves, croissants play fetch,
As muffin tops rise, a delightful sketch.

Wishing for magic, a cookie with flair,
But all that is left is an empty chair.
A pinch of this, a sprinkle there,
Turning dreams into ice cream, well, that's quite rare!

Yet, sprinkles of hope rain down from the sky,
With each drop of joy that tickles the eye.
As pretzels entwine in a comical dance,
The mirage of yearnings leads folks to prance.

So if you hear giggles around the stove,
Join in the fun, let your worries rove.
For every sweet dream is a slice of delight,
In mirages we find, a floating light.

Escaping the Ensnaring Thrum

The clock ticks loud, a mischief intent,
Whispers of time, so heartily spent.
Dancers in slippers, on steps out of tune,
Twirl past the cat, who's plotting a swoon.

A jester with bells sings tricks in the air,
While dogs in bowties dash here and there.
The music's a ripple, a silly old beat,
Leading us all to our own happy feet.

As shadows elongate and giggles grow strong,
We dodge the thrum, where we don't quite belong.
With whisks for wands, and pies for our hats,
We wriggle and wrangle, oh how the fun chats!

In mosaics of laughter, we flit and we chase,
The ensnaring thrum, we'll turn it to grace.
So bounce to the rhythm, let joy take a leap,
In the chaos of charm, we find what we keep!

Specters in a Shimmering Ball

At a ball where the shadows of muffins waltz,
Specters of sugar break bread, oh what faults!
Jelly jars twinkle, with clothes made of crumbs,
While cookies in gowns curtsy, oh how fun it hums!

Pies plop and plunder, they giggle with zest,
While forks play the fiddle, it's all just the best.
The chandeliers wobble, twinkling in delight,
As pasta performs with the grace of a kite.

With tea that sings and laughter that shines,
The dance floor is gleeful, where whimsy entwines.
As whispers of marshmallows dance up to the sky,
Here we find humor that makes spirits fly.

So if you should stumble upon this grand show,
Join in with the laughter, let your joy flow.
For in shimmering moments where silliness sprawls,
Are specters of fun in the heart of the halls.

Steps that Lead to Nowhere

Two left feet, I spin around,
My shoes all squeak with every sound.
The music plays, oh what a joke,
I trip and fall, then laugh and choke.

The floor is a maze, my mind a blur,
I dance like a crab, oh what a stir!
With each misstep, I gain some flair,
A circus act, without a care.

A partner slips, we both collide,
The joy is real, we cannot hide.
We whirl and twirl through silly schemes,
A laugh parade, or so it seems.

In jumbled steps, the night persists,
We'll dance and laugh, can't resist.
For life is fun when you don't know,
Just where those wild steps will go!

Veils of Delusion in the Moonlight

Moonlight twirls in sparkly beams,
I chase shadows, lost in dreams.
With fancy moves and glittered grace,
I dance with ghosts in this strange place.

A ghostly waltz, or so it feels,
I salute the moon, and then it squeals.
Veils of fabric dance like chatty birds,
They whisper secrets, all absurd.

Twirling round in tangled fancies,
I lead my feet on wild romances.
Each step I take is out of sync,
But who cares more? I laugh and wink.

The night giggles at my charade,
In this moonlit ball, I'm not afraid.
Chasing veils, I set my heart free,
In this grand show, it's just me!

Bound by the Siren's Echo

Oh, what a sound, can you hear that tune?
It lures me forth, under the moon.
The siren sings with silky pitch,
I follow close, oh what a hitch.

Each note's a chain that pulls me tight,
I shuffle haply into the night.
With wobbly steps, I start to prance,
The echoes lead me in a dance.

A fellow joins, with socks askew,
Together we sway to rhythms new.
With laughter bright, we lose our way,
What cares we have? Let's boogie, hey!

So bound we are by wails and cheers,
The strange song masks our silly fears.
In this ruckus, oh so sublime,
We'll dance and laugh throughout all time!

The Rhythm of Forgotten Whispers

Whispers float like feathers light,
I hear them murmur in the night.
They tickle ears and guide my feet,
In silly steps, I can't be beat.

They lead me back to step on air,
I sway and dip, without a care.
These forgotten tales take me high,
With laughter shared, we reach the sky.

In a jig that defies all laws,
I spin and twirl, with endless pause.
Each step I take is filled with glee,
The whispers giggle, just like me.

Let's dance away the hours lost,
In silly rhythms, we'll pay the cost.
For life's a jig, with playful quirks,
And in our dance, true magic lurks!

The Waltz of Deceptive Dreams

In a ballroom of whispers, we spin and glide,
Chasing shadows that dance, with nowhere to hide.
The music's a jest, the steps all a ruse,
Laughter erupts as we wear our bright shoes.

The partners we grab, with a twinkle in eye,
Are merely reflections of hopes passing by.
Round and round we go, like a merry-go-round,
Lost in our frolic, where sanity's drowned.

With each pirouette, a giggle we share,
In a world of mirages, we float in the air.
But the clock it does chime, and the dream goes askew,
As the punchline awaits, with its grandest debut.

So we leap to the moon, on a one-legged chair,
In a dance that's absurd, with a costumed affair.
Yet the smiles never fade, though the truth may disarm,
In the waltz of our hearts, there's always the charm.

Ethereal Chains Binding Hearts

In echoes of laughter, we twirl to the beat,
With glittering chains that feel oh-so sweet.
Caught in our folly, we hop and we skip,
Oh, who knew love could be such a trip?

A jester appears, with a wink and a grin,
Ties us together, oh where to begin?
With each playful tug, we reel and we sway,
As our heartstrings intertwine in their silly ballet.

On rollercoaster rides of romantic pretense,
We juggle our feelings, all for the suspense.
Winks from the crowd fuel our intricate game,
While we trip over words, but hey, who's to blame?

Yet amidst the chaos, the smiles take their hold,
In chains that are soft, not a whisper of cold.
For with every misstep, we giggle some more,
As we dance through this farce, leaving light at the door.

Labyrinthine Steps of Longing

Down winding paths that lead nowhere fast,
We skip in the maze, with echoes that last.
Chasing our tails, in a comical chase,
Where longing turns jesting, in this farcical space.

Each corner we turn, a surprise lies in wait,
With flip-flops and fumbles, oh isn't it great?
For we trip on our hopes, as we tango with fate,
In the skit of our hearts, there's no room for hate.

The walls whisper 'dance', while we waddle in sync,
With a croak and a giggle, all tied with a wink.
The exit seems far, yet the fun's in our feet,
As we sway with abandon, in this whimsical beat.

And so we embrace all the tangles and turns,
In the labyrinth of longing, where laughter now churns.
For what's life without jest, when the heart takes the lead,
In steps of delight, oh, we plant every seed!

The Twirl of Illusions Unveiled

Round and round the carousel spins with glee,
In costume of dreams, we all playfully flee.
Each spin is a secret, each turn holds a cheer,
As our shadows dance lightly, with naught but good cheer.

The curtain is lifted, revealing our plight,
With glimmers of laughter that sparkle so bright.
What if the truth is just part of the act?
In the theater of jest, we all play the fact.

We hop on the stage, where the chaos ignites,
As we dance through the night, in our comical flights.
With a wink and a flourish, we jive in delight,
In illusions unveiled, we embrace the sweet night.

So let's laugh at the tales that our hearts like to weave,
In the twirl of the making, we dare to believe.
For amidst all the fancies, the joy is the deal,
In this whirl of tomfoolery, our spirits in reel.

The Masquerade of Longing

Under masks we sway and twirl,
With dreams that give our hearts a whirl.
A jester's laugh, a kingly grin,
We all pretend, let the games begin.

In slippers made of golden thread,
We step on toes and laugh instead.
With every spin, we're lost in play,
Who needs the truth? Just dance away!

A waltz with shadows, dips so grand,
We forge our fate with a clumsy hand.
Each twinkling star, a playful tease,
Draws us to whimsy with the greatest ease.

A masquerade of dreams so bright,
As laughter leads us through the night.
In this grand ball, we'll never fall,
We keep our hopes, but hide them all.

Spirals of a Fading Truth

Round and round the tales we spin,
Where logic ends, the fun begins.
A twist of fate, a turn of glee,
Our minds are light, our spirits free.

In circles we chase the sparkling lie,
As questions flit like butterflies.
With each new loop, we giggle and sway,
Reality's just a game we play.

A riddle wrapped in giggles bright,
As truths dissolve in the moonlit night.
Onward we spiral, lost in the jest,
Life's a puzzle, but we love the quest.

So grab a partner, spin around,
In silly motions, we've finally found,
That truth is funny, hazy, absurd,
We laugh it off, as we've often heard!

Threads of Illusory Light

In glowing yarns, our hopes entwined,
A tapestry with secrets lined.
With every stitch, a giggle slips,
We weave our fancies, clumsy quips.

Like fireflies caught in a jar,
We play the fool, yet shine like stars.
Each flicker offers fleeting charm,
An illusion wraps us, safe from harm.

Beneath the glow, we dance and cheer,
As shadows bloom, we have no fear.
In threads of laughter, soft and bright,
We'll frolic on through endless night.

So let the patterns shift and sway,
We'll spin our dreams in the light of day.
For in this web, we come alive,
With every laugh, we learn to thrive.

Constellations of Make-Believe

Stars above us, cheeky and bold,
We paint our tales in shimmering gold.
A galaxy of giggles awaits,
In dreams we craft, no need for fates.

Planets whirl with a silly dance,
In comets' trails, we take a chance.
As we bounce through stardust and glee,
The universe laughs along with me.

Each constellation a tale so grand,
With whimsical critters, hand in hand.
They wink and nod from afar so bright,
Inviting us to play in the night.

So let us float on this cosmic ride,
In the realm of jest, we'll safely glide.
For in this sky, where dreams thrive,
We giggle and twirl, so very alive!

Choreography of the Fading Truth

In a world of twist and twirl,
Where the jester grins and swirls,
Bright colors hide the deeper shades,
And reason dances in charades.

Step left, then right, it's all a game,
Get your foot caught in the frame,
Round and round, we spin and sway,
Lost in laughter, come what may.

Lost socks found in jumbled spins,
The waltz of everyday wins,
With laughter loud and antics wild,
Reality skips, a playful child.

A puppet show of dreamer's glee,
Where truth is just a cup of tea,
With every step, the giggles grow,
In this circus we all know.

The Sway of Illusory Graces

Beneath the stage, a tangled mess,
Where giddy thoughts are dressed to impress,
The music plays, a comical call,
As we all pretend to know it all.

Twist on tiptoes, misstep in bliss,
What you thought was a waltz is a twist,
With every spin, we lose the beat,
And chuckle softly at our defeat.

Round we go, in clownish attire,
Shuffling steps fueled by desire,
The mirrors lie with cheeky grins,
Reflecting both losses and wins.

As we sway under moonlit glow,
The puppet strings begin to show,
Graced by folly, we all collide,
In this fancy, we can't abide.

Steps in the Hall of Reflections

In a hall where shadows prance,
Mirrors mimic every chance,
Two left feet bump and collide,
As giggles burst from deep inside.

Reflecting smiles, the truth is bent,
Each curve a jester's testament,
With a hop, a twirl, we juggle time,
Wobbling off in perfect rhyme.

Every faux pas, a gift indeed,
Spinning stories that few may heed,
Shattering moments, laughter bright,
We dance through wrongs, into the light.

In baffling steps and cheeky scope,
The dance floor's woven with dreams and hope,
Each awkward turn, a chance to glow,
Chasing shadows in splendid flow.

Surrendering to the Phantom's Tune

The specter winks, it's all in play,
With a tap and a spin, we sway,
In rhythm with a mischievous tease,
As echoes bounce on the evening breeze.

We surrender to whims, with giggles galore,
Where every step leads to more and more,
A jigsaw puzzle in silver shrouds,
Dancing with joy beneath the clouds.

In this ballet of laughter and cheer,
We tango with shadows, banishing fear,
Each misstep, a song in disguise,
As mirth fills the air and laughter flies.

With twirls and spins, we float away,
Caught in the rhythm where phantoms play,
In a whimsical whirl, we've all become,
Partners in folly, we laugh and hum.

Steps Echoing in a Silent Hall

Tiny feet in glitter shoes,
Twirl and spin, they can't refuse.
But in the mirror, a ghostly grin,
What a performance, where to begin!

A two-step here, a shuffle there,
With socks that slip and jumbled hair.
A solo act, yet no applause,
Just clumsy chaos without a cause!

The walls are silent, still in verse,
While I waltz like a curious purse.
Laughter echoes, a comical sight,
As shadows join in the moonlight.

Round and round, a dizzy spree,
Chasing echoes, just you and me.
A flat-footed jig in a grand hall,
How witty we are, in this fall!

Serenade of the Lost Illusions

Once upon a catchy tune,
Where dreams dance like a cartoon.
With every step, they pull away,
But oh, what fun in this cabaret!

A pirouette gone quite astray,
Falls into laughter, come what may.
The audience, a couch potato crowd,
Cheering wildly, 'Aren't we proud?'

Each jig a chuckle, each sway an art,
While shadows fumble at the start.
Who needs the stage, just call it fate,
When every twist is second rate!

Serenading lost little dreams,
With rhythms tangled as it seems.
In this folly, smiles persist,
Illusions that we can't resist!

Veils of Enchantment

A curtain flutters, oh what flair,
Hiding giggles beneath the air.
With gentle whispers, they begin to sway,
Veils of mystery at the end of the play.

A secret chime in shadows' glance,
Look at me, let's take a chance!
But all that glimmers can't bemuse,
When charm unravels like lost shoes.

Beneath these layers, laughter brews,
As I play a part in circus shoes.
Flicking veils, what could go wrong?
In a funny tale, we all belong.

With dance so lavish, the plot unwinds,
Oh what tricks are in our minds!
Behind each turn, we giggle loud,
Veils of dreams and a silly crowd!

Echoes of a Mirage

In the distance, a carnival glow,
With whispers of fun that surely flow.
But as I leap, the ground gives way,
Only to realize it's another play!

These echoes hide behind the fence,
Mimicking laughter, building suspense.
A dizzy rush in pixelated light,
Oh, what a prank, what a sight!

Mirages dance in the fading sun,
Chasing shadows, just for fun.
With every step, I float and glide,
While the real show prepares to hide.

So I tiptoe on this sugary dream,
Bouncing high on the fluffy cream.
What a ride, this tangled lore,
In the echoes where we long for more!

Mirage Beneath the Starlit Canopy

Beneath the twinkling lights we prance,
Chasing shadows, lost in chance.
Foolish laughter fills the night,
As dreams take wing and take to flight.

With each misstep, we spin around,
In a game where joy is found.
Hilarious antics, laughs to share,
Yet nobody seems to have a care.

Each twist, a giggle, each turn, a scream,
We juggle wishes, chase a dream.
As winks and nods lead us astray,
We dance like fools until the day.

Yet in this mirage, joy is true,
With playful hearts, we'll always renew.
Underneath the starlit dome,
We celebrate as if we're home.

The Jester's Elaborate Deceit

In a world spun by the jester's hand,
Wit and whimsy go hand in hand.
With painted faces, we fool and jest,
In the chaos, we find our best.

A flip, a flop, a tumble and roll,
Around the fire, we lose control.
Mixed up dreams, a wild charade,
All the world's a masquerade.

Juggling truths alongside a lie,
A sprinkle of laughter, oh my, oh my!
In the corners, giggles run free,
As charlatans dance with glee.

So raise a cup to the great charade,
With every jest, our worries fade.
In the folly, we find a way,
To turn the night into a play.

Twirls of the Dreambound Troupe

Round and round, the dreams take flight,
In a merry whirl, both day and night.
Painted smiles, and shoes so bright,
We jump into the colorful sight.

With every twirl, the world might shake,
A wink, a nod, for laughter's sake.
Twisted fables in rhymes we weave,
Each step we take, a prank to believe.

Mirrored faces, the fun won't cease,
As giggles rise, we find our peace.
Leaping figures in easy grace,
We frolic on in this wild place.

Let's spin a tale of joyful delight,
In this spectacle, we take flight.
With every leap, we toss away care,
In the twirls of dreams, we boldly dare.

Labyrinth of the Veil's Embrace

In the maze of laughter, we lose our way,
Chasing echoes that giggle and sway.
Masks remain, but hearts reveal,
The joy disguised, that's oh-so-real.

Each twist confounds, a jump and a shout,
In this riddle, we twist about.
Charmed by folly, we dance in time,
Instructors of humor, all things sublime.

Through corridors of whimsical cheer,
The veils pull back, laughter draws near.
With every turn, a ballad spins,
Where foolishness reigns, and mirth begins.

In the embrace of this playful ride,
We'll mock the shadows that try to hide.
With joy as our guide, we prance and race,
Finding delight in the maze's grace.

Dancing Shadows of the Mind's Eye

When shadows prance in moonlit glee,
A sneaky jig, a sight to see.
They trip and twirl with playful grace,
In a game of hide and seek they race.

Their laughs echo in the silvery night,
As they dodge the beams of spectral light.
One whispers, "I'll lead, you follow!"
But ends up doing the grandest swallow.

They salute the stars with clumsy style,
Each misstep brings a brand-new smile.
The night is young, their spirits high,
While the moon just chuckles in the sky.

In this whimsical waltz, let's all partake,
For the shadows hide no steps, just fate.
When the dawn breaks, oh what a spree,
We'll chase our dreams, as wild as can be!

The Illusive Cadence of Fate

In a ballroom where the clocks run fast,
A twist, a turn, the time won't last.
Each partner spins with a wink of the eye,
Their feet a blur beneath the sky.

They tango with the echoes of chance,
But nobody knows the true advance.
A misstep here, a laugh escapes there,
They're all just puppets in midair.

Whispers say, "Just follow the beat!"
But the melody's stuck on repeat.
So let's cha-cha with all our might,
In this silly dance through the night.

With every spin, confusion sets in,
While fate just giggles at our din.
We'll stumble through this raucous place,
While winking fate grins with glee on its face!

Spellbound in a Twisted Reverie

In a dream where the cats can talk,
With top hats on, they take a walk.
They prance along with a silly flair,
Pausing now and then for the air.

With each twist of the mind's own gear,
Comes a giggle or maybe a cheer.
The world's a stage, all in fun,
Like juggling apples under the sun.

Yet every step leads to a quirk,
A little fumble, a face of smirk.
Round and round, the laughter flows,
In this merry dance, anything goes.

As the night fades, dreams intertwine,
With every giggle, the stars align.
In this whimsical state we play,
Let's dance till the dawn takes us away!

The Enigma of the Woven Floor

Upon a floor where patterns converge,
Curly twirly paths make us surge.
Every step is a jigsaw, a quiz,
Where the answer's just as silly as this.

Wobbly waltzes lead us astray,
Yet somehow we're grooving anyway.
The tiles giggle beneath our feet,
Every misstep a comic feat.

Spinning and sliding, we take the stage,
While the floorboards laugh in a playful rage.
One dips the other, oh what a sight,
As the whole room erupts with delight.

In this enigma, we laugh like fools,
Chasing rhythm while changing the rules.
For the dance of life is trickier still,
Yet we'll sail through with humor and skill!

Whispers of the Veiled Masquerade

In masks we prance, oh what a sight,
With laughter loud, we dance in fright.
A twirl, a spin, then off we go,
Chasing shadows, what a show!

The jester slips upon the floor,
As giggles erupt, we beg for more.
In this charade, we lose our way,
Yet joy blooms bright, come what may!

The chandeliers wink, the curtains sway,
While silly faces brighten the fray.
With every step, a mishap's crown,
In this fine folly, we spin around!

Shadows on the Perpetual Stage

The spotlight's bright, but oh, so hot,
My pants fell down; was that the plot?
With every stumble, a chuckle breaks,
What nonsense, dear; 'tis just for kicks!

A slip, a slide, we charm and cheer,
The audience roars, oh what a sphere!
In shadows cast, we're clowns and kings,
The folly sings, as laughter rings.

Our lines get blurred, the script's askew,
But in this jest, we're all a crew.
The curtain calls, and down we go,
In fits of glee, we've stolen the show!

Echoes of the Enchanted Waltz

Two left feet, I take a chance,
In twirling skirts, I start to prance.
With every turn, my partner trips,
As giggles burst from silly lips.

The music swells, then stops, oh dear!
I bow too low, and lands near here.
A whirl, a twirl, the spin begins,
In this wild romp, we both just grin!

Around we go, the floor's now slick,
With flailing arms, we dance a trick.
In bright delight, we leap and sway,
In this grand farce, we'll dance all day!

Chains of the Celestial Riddle

Each step a puzzle in cosmic jest,
We laugh aloud, a grand quest.
With every chain, we float, we fling,
These knots of fate, how they sting!

The stars align, or do they trip?
As cosmic clowns, we lose our grip.
Wrapped in chains, but oh, so free,
In this riddle, we sway with glee!

Through galaxies of giggles bright,
We dance in dreams, through day and night.
With every twirl, our spirits rise,
In this fine folly, we touch the skies!

Illusion's Enticing Melody

A jig on my toes, oh what a sight,
The floor spins away, in morning light.
With socks that might slip, I'm caught in glee,
I trip on my dreams, oh let it be free.

Around me they swirl, this merry brigade,
With twirls and with hops, in bright masquerade.
The music it beckons, a laugh we all share,
As I dance with my shadow, without a care.

Oh look at my partner, what a fine show,
With two left feet, they steal my glow.
We twist and we turn, in chaotic delight,
Who needs quite the rhythm, when sparks feel so right?

So let's spin and whirl, to this silly refrain,
Each step is a giggle, no need for the pain.
With laughter that echoes, my heart sings aloud,
In a world full of whimsy, I'll dance with the crowd.

The Dance of Faded Echoes

In a room made of whispers, we skip and we sway,
Each giggle a flurry of night into day.
The echoes invite us to frolic and play,
While shadows march softly in a curious way.

Look at that fellow, with one shoe undone,
He spins like a top, oh, he thinks it's such fun!
But down he goes rolling, oh what a sight,
His laughter bursts forth, lighting up the night.

With a step to the left, and a hop to the right,
We trip on the rhythms that feel oh so light.
The walls clapped in time, as if they had feet,
While we chase down the ludicrous, oh so sweet.

Just a glance in the mirror, reveals quite the style,
With mismatched outfits, we dance with a smile.
So come join the frolic; life's too short, my friend,
In this funny charade, let's twist 'till the end.

A Gossamer Veil of Dreams

In a land made of wishes, we weave and we twine,
Amid frilly delights, our laughter's divine.
With whispers of secrets, the moon shines so bright,
Each dream is a waltz, a peculiar flight.

I spin like a pancake, then flop on the floor,
My companions burst out, they simply want more!
As giggles cascade, like a river of cheer,
We capture the hours, with no room for fear.

With ribbons of nonsense, we braid the night sky,
While friendly old clouds join to flutter on by.
In a carnival swirl, we dance on our toes,
Where the breeze joins our laughter, the sweet chaos flows.

Let's twirl with abandon, forget all the rest,
For in this fine moment, we're truly blessed.
The gossamer fabric of dreams all around,
Keeps us wrapped in the joy that we've gladly found.

Reflections in a Cracked Mirror

I glance at the shards, what a silly affair,
One side shows a grin, the other no hair!
A jigsaw of smiles, and each piece a joke,
As my doppelgänger dances, oh how we provoke.

With a twist and a shimmy, the faces collide,
In funhouse distortion, there's nowhere to hide.
We wink at ourselves, like pals in the fray,
In a carnival fun-time, we're the grand display.

The laugh lines we wear, all the evidence shows,
As we flit through the laughter, like petals that close.
With a step like a feather, and just enough flair,
Amid all this nonsense, we lighten the air.

So let's raise a glass to the quirky delight,
To the cracks in our mirrors that sparkle so bright.
With each hollow echo, our joy will endure,
In the playful reflections, we're happy, for sure!

www.ingramcontent.com/pod-product-compliance
Ingram Content Group UK Ltd.
Pitfield, Milton Keynes, MK11 3LW, UK
UKHW022104050225
454743UK00006B/71